WHY STRATEGIES FAIL

17 BLOOPERS
HOW TO SPOT THEM
AND HOW TO AVOID THEM

LAURENCE SMITH

A Chase Noble Management Guide
www.chasenoble.com

"Fantastic insight with a great creative streak."
Mark Adams, Chief Executive (fmr), Virgin Healthcare

"Innovation, creation, consultation, determination – just some of the reasons for success that Smith clearly identifies."
David Coleman, Group Chairman, Coleman & Company

"Strategy – derived from the Greek word for general – is about knowing where a company needs to be, then organising and leading so that others can deliver quickly and effectively. Smith has provided a concise guide to doing exactly that."
Colonel (retd) Tim Collins OBE

"I'm worried for Smith. His writing lacks the jargon, complexity and pretentiousness that are compulsory in this genre. Strategic insight should not be this accessible and entertaining. Other authors will be sticking pins in his wax effigy."
Graham Davies, author, The Presentation Coach

"Smith's strategy workshops have been hugely useful and informative; after heeding the advice, Posturite experienced tremendous growth."
Ian Fletcher-Price, Chief Executive, Posturite

"Smith's incisive ability to devise and articulate practical, value-added business solutions is at the heart of this book, which is packed with valuable advice."
Michael Grunberg, Chief Operating Officer, New Century

"For small business owners, this is a valuable and easy to follow resource, providing really useful tips at every point."
Grahame Jones, Founder, Soukias Jones Design

"Smith sweeps away the dust to give us an insightful, must-have guide to developing a sustainable strategy. Throw away every other strategy book you have ever bought."
Campbell Macpherson, author, In the Company of Leaders

"The thoughtful, intelligent and commercial approach Smith displays in his strategic work is reflected in this informative and entertaining read."
Nigel Marsh, Chief Executive, Medacs Healthcare

"This is brilliant. Smith's book is readable, practical and – most importantly – gives really good advice on developing a plan which is capable of being implemented."
Dermot Mathias, Senior Partner (fmr), BDO LLP, and Chairman (fmr), BDO International Policy Board

"Clarity and brevity are vital ingredients for a successful strategy. Smith follows that maxim in his readable, insightful manual."
Peter Owen, Operations Director (fmr), British Airways

"Strategic development requires analysis, vision, commercial acumen, practicality and wisdom. Smith displays all these attributes."
Simon Rhodes, EMEA Marketing Director, CBRE

"Smith possesses a flair for harnessing the power of an executive team to focus on the task at hand."
Dr Alexander Scott, Chief Executive, the Chartered Insurance Institute

"A great diagnostic roadmap for anyone embarking on a strategy review. There's something in almost every paragraph to highlight to your team."
Victoria Wallace, Chief Executive, Leeds Castle Foundation

This edition first published 2012.

Copyright © Chase Noble Ltd, 2012.

Chase Noble Management Guides is a trading name of Chase Noble Ltd.

Published by Chase Noble Ltd. Registered office Audley House, Brimpton Common, Berkshire RG7 4RT.

Illustrations by Kev F Sutherland.

Designed by Rita Sexton.

Printed by Keeps Printing, Newbury.

British Library Cataloguing in Publication Data. A catalogue record for this book is available from the British Library.

ISBN 978 - 0 - 9575092 - 0 - 7

CONTENTS

1   Muddling through. 01

2   Only the chairman speaks 05

3   Analysis overload. 09

4   Fluff not stuff 13

5   Wistful nostalgia 17

6   The king is dead. 21

7   Goodwill to all 25

8   Let's flee the state. 29

9   No bolder and no brighter. 33

10 Built to last ... for a bit 37

11 Busy fools 41

12 We don't do action. 45

13 Chaos theory. 49

14 Telepathy works (in sci-fi) 53

15 The ghost of Uncle Joe 57

16 On track. I think, at a guess, perhaps 61

17 It starts next month 65

ACKNOWLEDGEMENTS

Most of the organisations mentioned in this book, including every one of the *Best Practice In Action* examples, are known personally to me, and I'm grateful to all who were kind enough to approve the relevant references.

I have benefitted from working with numerous mentors and business leaders over the past couple of decades. There is insufficient space to acknowledge each by name, and it would be invidious to attempt a selection. Instead, I'd prefer to offer one simple all-encompassing thank you to the entire group.

Kev Sutherland is a renowned cartoonist and comedian, who added sizzle to each chapter with his repertoire of punchy illustrations. Rita Sexton is a phenomenal graphic designer, who used typography, layout and colour to create a tone for the book that's simultaneously professional and distinctive. Sarah Anderson reviewed the manuscript twice from her new abode down under, and provided dozens of valuable editorial suggestions. Each made an exceptional contribution, as did everyone else who offered comments and feedback along the way. I am in their collective debt.

I am fortunate to have a family that stoically accepts my lengthy absences on assorted consulting assignments. This book would have been impossible without their tolerance and support.

For this reason, and for many others, *Why Strategies Fail* is dedicated to Theresa.

... AND WHY STRATEGIES SUCCEED

AN INTEGRATED APPROACH TO AVOIDING BLOOPERS

You need a strategy

Engage your people

UNDERSTAND WHERE YOU ARE

CORE OPTIONS

≫ **Internal evaluation**
Strengths and weaknesses

≫ **External evaluation**
Opportunities and threats

UNDERSTAND WHERE YOU WANT TO BE

SET PRIORITIES

≫ Live in the future

≫ Respect your competitors

≫ Innovate to survive

≫ Customers pay your wages

≫ Government can make or break you

≫ Success must be sustainable

UNDERSTAND HOW TO GET THERE

DO IT, IN POWER TIME

≫ Get your teams aligned

≫ Communicate broadly, deeply, often

≫ Be flexible

≫ Measure your progress

FOREWORD

From Shakespeare to Star Wars, it is not the heroes but the iconic villains of fiction that exert the greatest pull on our imagination. We feel strangely attracted as we learn of their geneses, their schemes, their jealousies, their justifications. We wonder whether, but for precarious fortune and circumstance, we too would have followed a darker journey along life's pathway. "There but for the grace of God" is the chilling thought lurking deep within our consciousness.

In similar vein, the fear of failure haunts many chief executives. Only in part are they motivated by status and lucre. More often, it is the irresistible force of sheer paranoia that propels them to the hot seat. Once in authority, they are tormented with anguish lest they fall short, and end their days as a case study of wrong-headedness, ridiculed by peers, and exposed as vacuous charlatans.

The starting-point of this book is not why business strategies succeed, but why they fizzle, flop, flounder, fold and fail. It is based on many personal observations of catastrophe and hubris over 20 years.

But as C. S. Lewis teaches us, "Failures are finger posts on the road to achievement." I have been fortunate to work with many visionary executives who got the fundamentals spot-on. Whether leading renowned global corporations or thriving local businesses, they display an entrepreneurial knack for making the right call. So while "17 bloopers" are the vital organs of this book, I have also taken the opportunity to highlight best practice from a range of sectors – including private equity, consumer goods, philanthropy, financial services, property, and healthcare.

Some may notice a theme that runs throughout the book like an invisible thread. And that is the seductive lure of complacency. On the one hand, the firms I have chosen as exemplars of effective strategy have an instinctive enthusiasm for change, coupled with a restless appetite to excel. On the other lies the temptation to chill out; a satisfaction with reaching the peak, and an assumption the good times will roll forever. So, to all readers who are currently involved in a programme of strategic development, I wish you not simply good luck. But also freedom from complacency's whispering and insidious voice.

Laurence Smith, Berkshire, 2012

MUDDLING THROUGH 01

YOU NEED A STRATEGY

- We live in an era of rapid economic, technological, regulatory and consumer change

- Many businesses, overwhelmed and at the mercy of events, concentrate on muddling through

- Other businesses resolve to take control, shaping their own future

- The first rule of strategic planning is to have one

Before the Industrial Revolution, most people spent their entire existence within a few miles of their place of birth. And the world was largely unchanged from when they entered it, to when they left it.

Some might find reassurance in stability; others may regard it as tedious beyond measure. In any event, such times are long gone. We live in an era of rapid economic, technological, regulatory and consumer change.

When the new millennium dawned, who could have foreseen the scale of changes the next decade would witness? A decade in which America would suffer the world's most devastating terrorist attack, much of the United Kingdom's banking sector would fall into public ownership, and a man with the name Barrack Obama would hold the most powerful elected office on the planet.

The pace of change has not let up for decades. The National Science Foundation, surveying recent breakthroughs in medicine, engineering and information technology, estimates that between 80 and 90 per cent of the scientists who have ever lived are alive today. There is more processing power on the average laptop than in the Apollo 11 mission that sent Neil Armstrong and Buzz Aldrin on their 500 million mile round trip to the moon.

How should businesses respond to these seismic events? Should they play defence, like the underdog team at the final of a major sporting contest, burning up their reserves of energy to keep the score line respectable while their opponents take the initiative? Or should they play offence, and seize control of the game?

Many firms, overwhelmed by the pace of change, simply concentrate on muddling through. William Rees-Mogg, former editor of *The Times*, calls this the "Picnics on Vesuvius" attitude – ignoring upheavals in the surrounding landscape that threaten to disturb the status quo.

As change becomes more intense, such firms find themselves buffeted by forces beyond their control. They duck and dive, desperate to reach the month-end intact. They persevere with their horse-and-carriage operation until the final possible moment, shutting their eyes to the onset of the automobile. They are at the mercy of events.

TAKING CONTROL

The other option is to embrace change. The instinct of these firms is to shape their own destiny, setting the pace for others to follow. They visualise what their future should be, and take positive steps to make it happen. Their mode of operation is to act, not to react.

Strategists are firmly in this second camp. Their conviction is that, in turbulent times, muddling through is not an option. Taking control during a period of change is at the heart of every winning strategy.

For many firms, taking control means the aggressive exploitation of new opportunities. Their priority may be to dominate sectors where they are already active. Alternatively, they may be pursuing growth into adjacent sectors, or the acquisition of competitors, or the creation of a suite of innovative products and services. In each case, their strategy is one of expansion.

I began my working life with two business services firms for whom taking control was second nature. Accountants *Stoy Hayward* could have been marginalised by the muscle of the "big brand auditors" on the one hand, and local book-keepers on the other. Instead, they carved a unique service, perfectly matched to supporting the growth of entrepreneurial businesses around the globe. They were prime movers in the formation of the international BDO network, attracting the loyalty of entrepreneurs with global aspirations. And they developed a portfolio of complementary services such as corporate finance, risk management, and franchising contracts, so that clients would not be tempted elsewhere when they required different types of advice.

The advertising agency *Ogilvy and Mather* (now part of the WPP media group) displayed a similar "let's go for it" attitude. By the mid 1980s, advertising had matured as a profession. Clients were more informed and analytical, demanding campaigns that built their revenue lines rather than simply winning prestigious awards. Ogilvy and Mather became pioneers in the measurement of advertising effectiveness. Audience research became central to the advertising process. Account executives were recruited with commercial experience. New production methods were developed that enabled creative treatments to be adapted faster. And the firm invested in the UK's biggest direct marketing resource, led by Drayton Bird, whose obsession with advertising metrics revealed insights about consumer behaviour that had previously been subject to guesswork.

Of course, taking control does not always take the form of rising sales. Strategies do not inevitably build towards a sunlit tomorrow. For some firms, taking control means retrenchment, downsizing, the elimination of unprofitable product lines, and the sale of non-core assets. In fact, in a climate of economic austerity, the strategic priorities for many firms are to live within their means, maintain a steady bottom line, and sidestep oblivion. These are perfectly legitimate choices to pursue.

While the content of such strategies may vary, the underlying philosophy is the same. First, by taking deliberate steps, on a timeline of its own choosing, a firm avoids the indignity of having unpleasant decisions thrust upon it when no other options are available. Second, consciously building an organisation that is geared and relevant for the next decade increases the likelihood of being around to experience and enjoy it.

So, the first rule of strategic planning is to have one.

BEST PRACTICE IN ACTION

POSTURITE

Posturite offers a range of products and educational services to cut the cost of work absenteeism relating to musculoskeletal disorders.

It was established by entrepreneur Ian Fletcher-Price when he left London's financial heartland in the mid-1990s, and for a number of years lived a hand-to-mouth existence. During a strategic planning exercise in 1998, all aspects of the business were systematically reviewed, including the product range, the marketing activities, the customer base, and the competitive landscape.

Three strategic priorities were agreed to deliver a step change in Posturite's scale and market impact. Within years, Posturite was established as the dominant player in the sector. In 2011, the firm was turning over £12 million, employing over 100 staff across the UK.

ONLY THE CHAIRMAN SPEAKS
02

ENGAGE YOUR PEOPLE

- When large corporations emerged, strategic responsibility began and ended with the board of directors

- Employee participation is vital in crafting a robust and grounded strategy

- A range of structured and ad hoc tools can be deployed to engage staff at all levels

- The workforce is also an essential stakeholder when firms define their core values

When large corporations emerged in the early twentieth century, responsibility for strategy unambiguously rested with the board of directors.

Two General Motors executives, James Mooney and Alan Reiley, developed a series of ground rules for organisational effectiveness, based upon practices that seemed to operate effectively in the military and the Roman Catholic church. The heart of their approach was the scalar principle, which emphasised hierarchical authority. It described the division – almost a chasm – between the roles of the board (to design strategy) and of the management team (to deliver operationally).

Mooney and Reiley's ideas had the virtue of being neat and orderly, and they were influential for a time. But ultimately, they could not survive their inevitable collision with reality. Some firms still hold the view that corporate plans are devised by very important people, sequestered in dark rooms, and then imposed on the masses. But not many, and such firms tend not to prosper.

In modern complex economies, the creation of strategy requires far greater sophistication. Throughout large firms, individuals in many different roles will hold information, views and perspectives that can inform the strategic process. Some people will interact daily with customers, some with suppliers, some with regulators, and some with shareholders. All these dealings are a potential goldmine of insights. They may give early warning of problems to be resolved. They may highlight emerging segments of the market that have unique needs. Or they may reveal aggressive activity by a competitor that poses a severe threat to market share.

The planning process needs to corral and marshal all this valuable intelligence. It needs to provide channels through which it can be sifted, scrutinised and tested. It needs actively to engage people throughout the organisation.

Wider engagement may simply provide renewed momentum for strategies already underway. Or it may suggest issues that can best be addressed through a change in direction. Almost always, it will help to construct a more potent strategy than would otherwise be in place.

Many processes can be used to engage staff in strategic planning. Some are finely structured, others are more spontaneous. They range from suggestion boxes, to surveys, to representative forums, to brainstorms, to focus groups. Leaders who are determined to create robust, relevant strategies will often use facilitated workshops to battle-test their initial hypotheses. They will share with staff the direction they are proposing to follow, and ask their people to rip it apart; to argue why it may be the wrong course and could lead to oblivion. Having exposed potential flaws, the moderator then invites staff to help rebuild and reconstruct, so the strategy is as relevant as possible to the challenges they are directly experiencing.

Regardless of the tools, efforts to engage the workforce only yield results if staff are convinced their input is taken seriously. When they recognise their contributions are benefiting the company's long-term fortunes, the quality and depth of insight is likely to rise in subsequent years.

CORE VALUES

The strategic process is, of course, not the only way to engage the workforce in corporate success. Firms are increasingly asking their people to help define their core values – the principles that bind them together, and endure regardless of year-to-year priorities. Values such as honesty, service, optimism, community, or financial responsibility are common in leading organisations. In the views of many pioneering chief executives, simply-expressed but deeply-rooted values make a tangible difference to the health of their company.

Thomas Watson Jnr, who led IBM for 30 years and oversaw its transformation into an international icon, stated: "The single most important factor in corporate success is faithful adherence to your core beliefs."

Watson lit upon an important truth. Agreeing a statement of values is essential, but is also the easy stage. The next step is for managers and staff to bring them to life, and apply them to real business situations. While strategies are continually refreshed to address new challenges, core values, once articulated, can endure for decades. Their combination creates a potent mix of stability and adaptability, encouraging a shared culture and informing decision-making. If a major customer threatens litigation, or a media fiasco occurs, or a whistle-blower in a remote office threatens to expose malpractice, then people within the organisation have a common frame of reference with which to judge their response.

When staff members sense the firm's core principles and future course have emerged in part from their own experience, the strategy ceases to be an abstract concept, impenetrable to all, removed from the real world. On the contrary, it becomes firmly grounded. It will be visible to those outside the firm – expressed in the handling of customer service calls, or the wording of e-mail communications, or the application of aftercare policies. This is strategy coming alive, through thousands of unique interactions, every hour of the day.

THE CHARTERED INSURANCE INSTITUTE

The Chartered Insurance Institute (CII) is the professional body for insurance practitioners in the United Kingdom and worldwide.

Every year, staff throughout the organisation are actively encouraged to develop ideas and recommendations by holding structured interviews with external organisations – such as corporate insurers, consumer groups, or other professional bodies. The insights that emerge are then fed into the planning process. For example, video highlights of staff suggestions form the opening sequence of the annual directors strategy away day.

Alongside strategy development, staff workshops take place throughout the year to discuss the CII's four values (teamwork, customer focus, innovation, integrity), and how they can be used to positive effect. The multi-layered nature of staff engagement in these vital matters was one reason that the CII was recently awarded the Gold Standard by Investors In People.

ANALYSIS
OVERLOAD
<u>03</u>

UNDERSTAND WHERE YOU ARE

- An internal evaluation involves turning a ruthless spotlight on all aspects of the organisation's operations

- An external evaluation reviews the environmental players and agencies whose activities have a bearing on the firm's fortunes

- Each assessment should be undertaken open-mindedly, informed by reliable data, and not used to defend established practices

- The conclusion is a shortlist of options to capitalise on strengths, minimise weaknesses, exploit opportunities, and mitigate threats

Entrepreneurs often have a profound, meticulous understanding of the situation wherein they find themselves. This is why, even if they don't commit it to a lengthy written document, they can be brilliant intuitive strategists. Making a balanced, reasoned and insightful diagnosis of the current situation is critical to the development of an effective strategy. Firms cannot begin to consider "where they want to be" until they fully comprehend "where they are".

Entrepreneurs have a natural advantage in reaching a rounded assessment: they are, of necessity, generalists. A typical day might see them dealing in turn with sceptical financiers, belligerent regulators, litigious suppliers, defecting staff, exuberant customers, and forensic technicians. This spread of activity places entrepreneurs in a privileged position. They can connect the dots. They can create threads between facts that might otherwise remain locked in silos. They will perceive themes that are invisible to functional managers, whose view is constrained by rigid organisational boundaries.

As for the entrepreneur, so it is for all strategists. Phase one, "understanding where you are", involves assembling the widest range of material onto the largest possible canvas – with one side of it relating to internal capabilities, the other to the external environment.

The internal evaluation turns a ruthless spotlight on all aspects of the firm's operations. The scope may encompass its financial performance, its products and services, its marketing and sales activities, its procurement, its systems and its human resources (the "basic building blocks" of the organisation). Analysis may delve into the percentage of total profit represented by each product in a portfolio, or the utilisation rates of key assets, or the changing effectiveness over time of marketing channels, or the firm's ability to attract and retain high calibre graduates. Once complete, the internal evaluation forms the basis for understanding key strengths and weaknesses.

The external evaluation studies the various players and agencies in the wider environment whose behaviour has a bearing on the firm's success. This review will typically extend to the customers, competitors, suppliers, potential entrants, and substitutes. Harvard Business School guru Michael Porter, influential author of *Competitive Strategy* and *Competitive Advantage*, famously labelled these the "five forces". Vital questions may include the level of dependence upon monopolistic or duopolistic suppliers, or the ability of customers to switch away, or the unit costs incurred by competitors through their offshore production. The external evaluation illuminates the nature of key opportunities and threats.

In each case, strategists undertake their research open-mindedly, not using it to defend established practices and entrenched interests. Cold and unyielding data must be allowed to intrude. Strategic conclusions need solid foundations.

Shortly after privatisation, *British Airways* decided to review its non-core support services, such as catering, facilities, print and stationery, and ground vehicle operation and maintenance. The exercise was informed throughout by assembling and interpreting data that had been hidden away for years. Under state ownership, British Airways' support services were run as cost centres within the monolithic corporation. Now, with greater management freedom, fresh options could be considered, including outsourcing, joint venturing, enhancements to the current operations, and profit centre status providing services to third party airlines at London's hub airports. Given the headcount and cost involved, any decision needed to be driven by empirical, objective data, rather than executive caprice. The service quality and cost-effectiveness of each support service was rigorously benchmarked against best market practice and plotted on a three-dimensional scale before a determination was made. As a result, British Airways made decisions that stood up to solid scrutiny.

INFORMATION INTO INSIGHT

Sometimes, existing sources cannot provide the facts that strategists need. Lateral thinking may be needed to obtain them. For example, bespoke computer simulations can be used to produce tailored analysis. Mystery shopping can give a truer flavour of the customer experience. Direct observation can be made of competitor activity (some firms have been known to station people outside their competitors' factories, counting the number of trucks that depart). If all else fails, frontline managers may be asked to use their experience and make subjective judgements. To understand the orders-of-magnitude of key issues, strategists will often need to use their imagination, and triangulate contributions from multiple independent sources.

Data collection is a necessary, but insufficient, component of the "where we are" phase. Once the facts are gathered, the strategist must use them to ask awkward questions, repeatedly using the phrase "so what…?" to test their relevance and truth. As with the best detective fiction, penetrating questioning can lift the fog and reveal hard facts.

So, from the internal evaluation, strengths and weaknesses have been derived. From the external evaluation, opportunities and threats have been identified. Together, these comprise a SWOT statement (strengths, weaknesses, opportunities, threats).

Literal entrepreneurs place their own capital at risk. Corporate entrepreneurs build businesses inside an established listed company. The common bond is that talented strategists of all kinds use the SWOT to capitalise on strengths, minimise weaknesses, exploit opportunities, and mitigate threats. They display the naked instinct to hone in on commercially attractive strategic options – from pinpoint fine-tuning, to a radical new direction – that benefit their market position.

At this point, a pulsating glow may be detectable in the strategists' eyes.

EQUITY RED STAR

Equity Red Star began life as a Lloyd's motor insurer in 1946, and is now one of the top six personal lines insurers in the country.

In 2005, under the heading "shaping up for the future", Equity Red Star undertook a full review of every one of its 14 business lines, from the mainstream (private cars and household), to the specialist (such as vans, agricultural, taxis, haulage). In each case, it collected statistical and perceptual data from brokers and customers.

Levels of awareness were studied, as were levels of satisfaction with product design, pricing, and claims support. Armed with this wealth of material, Equity Red Star was able to make informed decisions at strategic and product line levels, building on strengths and addressing areas of potential vulnerability.

FLUFF NOT STUFF 04

UNDERSTAND WHERE YOU WANT TO BE

- Key elements of the strategy begin to emerge and coalesce from the SWOT analysis

- A mission statement is the strategy's beating heart, and objectives turn bluster into beef

- Winning strategies deliver the goals, and often need to be game-changing

- The strategy must create value, for example in the form of shareholder returns

Some children have a natural flair for the piano. Others could struggle through one-to-one tuition from a maestro for a year without hitting a right note. And some chief executives experience a similar blindspot when asked to articulate the firm's long-term direction. They may be able to chair meetings, bark orders, and admonish under-performers, but they cannot raise sights beyond the immediate horizon. They cannot point to the promised land.

The most charismatic leaders describe the future in terms so vivid and compelling they create a virtual timewarp. Their followers feel almost able to reach out and touch the prize, as if it exists today. Once again, entrepreneurs set the standard. It may be early days; they may not have raised a penny of funding, or built a prototype. But they can communicate their destiny as if they were looking directly at it. They talk with clarity and passion about the people who will, years ahead, choose to purchase their products and services. They detail with precision the irresistible experience such customers will enjoy.

For strategists, this is phase two of the development programme. Having set out the challenges of "where we are", the next exercise is to forge solutions; to determine "where we want to be."

A mission statement is, classically, the strategy's beating heart. It summarises the business concept, the value being proposed to customers, and the capabilities that will set the organisation apart from its peers. It aims to encapsulate volumes of thinking and insight in, typically, no more than 25 words. The statement should be both aspirational and credible. Vague platitudes, capable of multiple interpretations, are counter-productive. But an inspiring, clear statement of the intended trajectory is corporate gold dust.

The objectives turn bluster into beef. Sitting alongside the mission statement, they quantify the desired outcomes. They provide measures against which performance can be evaluated. They scream "no sanctuary for drifters, no place for second-raters to hide away. This organisation knows exactly what it wants to achieve".

The strategies are the key initiatives that deliver stated goals. They are the end-result of savage filtering. The phase one SWOT analysis tends, by its nature, to be an expansive process. It often features open-ended brainstorming sessions, where outlandish ideas are encouraged by moderators who say, "Today, there is no such thing as a bad suggestion!" They conclude with sheets of flipchart paper hanging from the rafters, submerged with post-it notes on which hundreds of contradictory possibilities have been randomly scribbled – perhaps local market ascendancy, launching into South America, leapfrogging into new niches, luring talent from the rest of the sector with a bonus bonanza, or acquiring dozens of regional players who are convulsed by poor cashflow. Now, in phase two, key strategies must emerge and coalesce through applying the disciplines of precision and closure. After the merits of the myriad opportunities have been weighed, brutal selections must be made. "Convergence" is an ungainly word, which appears in many top 10 lists of the worst business jargon, but it symbolises precisely how the process must end.

No chief executive should introduce the strategies with the phrase: "Here are the 28 bullet-points you need to remember." Three ideas are ample, which is how Churchill was able to motivate a nation by promising nothing more than blood, sweat and tears, and how Julius Caesar could summarise his short war with Pharnaces II in the city of Zela with the phrase "veni, vidi, vici".

GAME-CHANGING

Winning strategies often need to be game-changing. Only so much can be achieved by organically enhancing the status quo. W Chan Kim and Renee Mauborgne, directors of the Blue Ocean Strategy Institute, argue that successful firms create uncontested market space and make the competition irrelevant. They refuse to engage in cut-throat rivalry that squeezes margins to a whisper. Instead they identify untapped demand, redefining customers' value expectations, and justifying widening margins. They illustrate the "game-changing" concept with the case history of Cirque du Soleil. Faced with a sector – the circus – dominated by Barnum and Bailey, and where attendances were spiralling downwards, they went back to first principles, and forged a new concept of the circus experience that melded together practices such as spectacular storytelling, drama and lighting, that were borrowed from the worlds of theatre, cinema, opera and ballet.

A strategy must, of course, create value. In traditional, commercial enterprises, this takes the form of shareholder returns. There may be a liquidity event, such as the sale of the business on the financial markets or to a strategic partner. The share price may climb on the back of rising dividends. Or the company may initiate a stock buy-back programme once it has sufficient cash reserves. For some investors, it will be important to understand the degree of risk associated with a strategic direction, so they can ensure it is consistent with their own risk appetite. Owners will rightly grow frustrated with strategies that are providing secure employment for executives, and trainloads of new projects to be financed, without returning a red cent.

Demonstrating a direct link between the course being chartered, and the value of an investor's holdings, is yet another addition to the lengthening list of obligations that fall upon the shoulders of the effective strategist.

SIMS GROUP

SIMS Group is the leader in reproductive medicine in Ireland, providing fertility treatment from a hi-tech clinic in Clonskeagh, Dublin.

During a strategic review exercise in 2012, it set out the specific objectives that would enable it to maintain a leadership position. It would operate a unique business model combining a range of services within one group, offering a seamless journey to customers from initial consultation to pregnancy.

It would grow its core services organically in Ireland, through referral networks, press relations and awareness-raising. It would enter into new geographical markets for its core in vitro fertilisation (IVF) service. And it would opportunistically seek to grow into adjacent areas of specialism. Where appropriate, growth would be underpinned by strategic partnerships or joint venture based contracts.

WISTFUL NOSTALGIA
<u>05</u>

LIVE IN THE FUTURE

- Strategists must be alert to wider historic events

- The changing pattern of wealth distribution across the globe is the dominant theme of our times

- Technology is revolutionising practices of communication, healthcare, leisure and retail

- Business leaders must shape their products, services and organisations to fit the world of 2020 and beyond

"We are living through the end of 500 years of western ascendancy" observes historian Niall Ferguson in his ground-breaking exposition on the emergence of China as an economic juggernaut.

In just 30 years, he calculates, the ratio of per capita Gross Domestic Product in China compared with the United States has risen from 4 per cent to 19 per cent, as it diversifies rapidly away from a low-cost production industrial base. Measures of educational attainment in academically rigorous subjects such as mathematics and science reveal a widening gulf between the performance of students in Southeast Asia and the "European laggards". With research and development expenditure up sixfold in a decade, the nature of Chinese society is changing before our eyes. Recently, it overtook America as the world's largest automobile market, and a Pew Research survey found that 47 per cent of Americans now regard China as the world's leading economic powerhouse.

The shifting distribution of wealth across the globe is the dominant trend of our times. But it is not the only one. The demographic profile of western societies has also been changing, and the social make-up of Europe 10 or 20 years from now can be forecast with reasonable confidence. Increasing life expectancy means that populations are ageing, with new entrants to the workplace fighting for scarce employment against people in their grandparents' cohort who are seeking to forestall retirement. There is a far greater ethnic mix, especially in large cities, which have become melting pots of different languages, faiths, arts and cuisines, and where second-generation immigrants now have dual cultural allegiances. Women are securing equal status in the workplace, challenging customs and worldviews that were once accepted without question in male-orientated times. The great urban conurbations thrive at the expense of the countryside, acting like honey to ambitious worker-bees. And only a minority of households now exhibit the traditional family structure, with more adults deferring marriage, avoiding marriage, or re-marrying.

Turning from demography to technology, we see working practices being revolutionised in both mature and developing economies. In communications, letters affixed with postage stamps and dropped into the mailbox have long been surpassed by e-mail. In leisure, more music is now purchased digitally than in disc form. In healthcare, medical practitioners are concerned with sickness prevention and the management of illness, not simply with elective procedures that treat and cure. In retail, a generation has grown accustomed to purchasing clothing, hardware and gifts without leaving the comfort of the living room.

In macro-economics, government budgets are facing unprecedented pressure. Austerity measures are being enacted throughout Europe, with some programmes – such as defence and welfare – disproportionately affected. Most national exchequers seem to have reached the limit of their ability to tax, with internationally mobile corporations and individuals shunning countries that levy taxes they deem excessive. And with a reducing proportion of the population being of working age, the seeds of inter-generational conflict are being sown everywhere.

Conscious of the planet's limited resources, consumers actively seek brands they regard as responsible custodians. Broadcast documentaries and specialist websites raise awareness of the damage to air quality, forestry, coastal waterways, and wildlife from bad business practices. Purchasing decisions become more nuanced than simply assessing cost versus value.

Within education, the university experience is barely recognisable to pre-2000 alumni. The spectre of tuition fee repayment means students spend more time engaged in learning than propping up the dormitory bar. But, more broadly, classroom instruction itself has evolved. It is now supplemented with online resources, podcasts and chatrooms, with game-based activities and learning analytics. Student assessment is more continuous, focusing on application and judgement not simply assimilation and memorisation. In a recent study, 93 per cent of American teachers agreed that blended learning tools improve impact.

ADAPT TO THRIVE

Successful strategists must be alert to these historic events. They cannot retreat to a bunker, and hope to ignore them. Firms that are insensitive to the march of history will be swept aside. Of America's 10 largest companies in 1955 by headcount, only two (General Electric and AT&T) still made the list half a century later. The rest – one-time giants of industry such as US Steel, Chrysler, Amoco, Goodyear and Firestone – had variously collapsed, shrunken or been taken over, replaced on the list by Wal Mart, UPS, Hewlett Packard and the Bank of America; firms more effectively positioned for a knowledge and service-based economy.

Businesses must be ready to exploit trends, fashion and bandwagons – the entire raucous cacophony that is transforming society from its roots. Leaders cannot linger nostalgically in a world that has passed. The History Channel has carved an admirable media niche, but strategists should escape its temptations. Reinforcing this point, some companies now employ a resident futurologist, whose singular purpose is to stress-test every aspect of the operation in the glare of tomorrow's challenges.

Corporate behemoths rise and fall when they are able – or not – to predict trends and reinvent themselves. The dinosaurs roamed the earth for around 160 million years. They were perfectly adapted to their environment, but faced extinction as soon as it was displaced.

Employing a next generation mentality, business leaders must shape their products, services and organisations to fit the world of 2020 and beyond. The strapline "adapt to thrive" should be indelibly stamped across the forehead of any budding strategist.

BEST PRACTICE IN ACTION

ENVEST VENTURES

Envest Ventures is an early stage private equity investment fund based in Virginia, United States.

Its investment selection criteria are geared towards businesses that leverage long-term trends within society. Over the years, its portfolio has included technology that assists the remote monitoring of intensive care patients; a next generation defence contractor; an international tax franchisor; a Microsoft partner; a molecular technologies incubator; and a business providing medical treatment to the frail elderly.

Applying this philosophy to its investment strategy, Envest has achieved a net annual rate of return of 22.3 per cent over 10 years, placing it as a top-performing 2000-vintage year fund.

THE KING IS DEAD

06

AVOIDING BLOOPERS:
CUSTOMERS PAY YOUR WAGES... AND HAVE CHOICES

- The power balance between providers and clients has been reversed by the internet

- Segmentation is no longer an esoteric term; it is now at the epicentre of strategic analysis

- Marketing budgets are refocusing from foghorn advertising to building communities of interest

- Well-managed relationships with high value customers are a remarkable strategic asset

A paradox of our times is that, as executives rise through the ranks, so the degrees of separation multiply between them and their customers. Their assumptions about customers' needs and attitudes grow outdated at best, if not wholly misplaced, as their direct contact diminishes.

If strategists ever had the luxury of treating customers as an after-thought, such days are gone forever. The internet has reversed the power balance in the provider-client relationship. Healthcare professionals complain that, every day, patients sit in consultation rooms having already completed an online self-diagnosis, and printed out reams of Wikipedia pages listing their prescription options. For doctors, such transparency may be unwelcome. For the rest of the population, it is liberating; demystifying arcane subjects that were once the preserve of a privileged elite.

From basic office stationery suppliers to the construction of new homes, customers have free access to real-time information on pricing and product options with just a handful of browser clicks. Such knowledge no longer demands weeks of painstaking phone calling and research. Whole swathes of the economy have become more open due to high speed broadband internet.

Strategies that rely on consumer inertia are inoperable. Customers use social networking to share their experiences. With greater awareness of what constitutes "best-in-class", expectation levels soar remorselessly. Bells-and-whistles are introduced, but their life cycle is compressed. Features that once delighted customers are now dismissed as the minimum acceptable standard. Airbags and music systems are no longer bespoke extras to negotiate during a car purchase; they are integrated into the core product. Blackberries were once the height of novelty for travelling and time-pressured executives; today they are almost quaint in their functional limitations.

In every sector, technology has eliminated the hassle and trauma of switching. A minor service disruption can be sufficient provocation for consumers to lose patience and test the market. Cyberspace overflows with websites whose singular proposition is to ease the seamless movement of customers from one provider to another.

Yet, properly managed customer relationships can be a remarkable strategic asset. In *Customer Connections*, Robert Wayland and Paul Cole explore a number of practical ways for strategists to move customers to the heart of the corporate journey. All organisations, they suggest, must begin by understanding the value of their customer portfolio. Does the profitability of individual clients congregate closely around the mean, or is there huge variance between the most and least valuable? Where loss-making customers are identified, can the value be actively managed upwards or outwards? And how can high-value customers be embraced – can they perhaps be invited to participate in the process of product development? Vitally, the natural instinct of a high-value customer is to reject the offer of a one-size-fits-all product or service. They demand something finely tailored to their personal needs.

SEGMENTS AND COMMUNITIES

Customer segmentation was once an esoteric practice of direct marketers, who varied the text on leaflet door drops depending on the categorisation of residential homes in a district, or tweaked the photography on mail shots to reflect the age profile of the recipients. Increasingly, segmentation also preoccupies the mind of the strategist, perhaps aware from bitter experience that offering one product to everyone means providing it to no one. A personal mission for such people should be coaching the top management team to be customer-driven and segment-led.

We see segmentation practiced by satellite broadcasters. The four terrestrial channels to which Britons were restricted in the last century have morphed into hundreds, each catering for a minority interest or taste. Traditional cola cans are now retailed alongside giant size, family packs, mini packs, cherry flavour and diet, each appealing to a unique demographic. Eighty thousand Wembley spectators watch the same sporting event, but their experience is packaged and sold in dozens of ways, depending on whether they are classified as a corporate host, a cash-strapped fan, or an impulse purchaser.

Aware of these issues, many chief executives are refocusing their marketing budgets from foghorn advertising, to targeted customer research and communication. Many consumer brands now facilitate web-based communities of interest. The firm becomes the enabler, hosting a secure and moderated environment in which different categories of customer can meet and interact with others sharing the same interests. Some chief executives mandate that their entire executive team, from finance to secretariat, must participate in these communities, setting for each one personal objectives that include significant, direct exposure to the firm's customer base.

Wherever customers are wont to exercise with abandon their freedom to choose, there is a litmus test that strategists must apply before proceeding with the corporate plan: Do high-value customers, inspecting the range of products on offer, see an indistinguishable morass of impractical features which "my ancestors might have liked"? If so, then it is time for the firm to reclaim the drawing board from the attic, and shake off the musty thicket of cobwebs.

BEST PRACTICE IN ACTION

ZURICH

Zurich International Life is a global provider of investment solutions for internationally-mobile, as well as locally domiciled, high net worth individuals.

It runs a number of insight programmes to ensure it is fully aware of the attitudes, expectations and concerns of many categories of customers. Research activities involve web surveys, telephone interviews, face-to-face interviews, and moderated focus groups. They can be broad in scope, allowing the customers to set the agenda, or focused upon one or two hypotheses which Zurich wishes to test. Whenever Zurich seeks to increase its presence in a territory, customer insight will be a prerequisite to investment.

In recent years, focus groups in cities as diverse as Taipei, Barcelona, Dubai and Singapore have influenced decisions on product design through to communications.

GOODWILL TO ALL
07

AVOIDING BLOOPERS:
PREPARE FOR A WARZONE

- At its most raw, strategy is about "how to take on your competitors … and win"

- When markets are flat-lining, firms primarily pursue growth at the expense of their rivals

- Competitive advantage can be secured through differentiation, or through lowest cost provision

- Once a competitive strategy is defined, the implications permeate every corner of the business

A favourite gambit of professors at London Business School, when lecturing a class of freshmen, is to ask the room to consider a definition of strategy. The penny drop moment comes when, after taking suggestions for a number of minutes, the lecturer points out that not a single student has made reference to *competition*. This, the teacher will argue, is a startling omission. In one pithy phrase, it will be proposed, strategy is about nothing more than "how to take on your competitors … and win".

Whenever they make a purchase, consumers use imaginary but finely-tuned scales to balance the advantages of competitive offerings. The costlier the ticket, the more time they will spend comparing the features across a broad expanse of alternative providers. Often there can be just one winner, meaning the final decision is merciless. A typical consumer needs just a single washing machine, or motorcycle, or hat stand, or garden shed. There is no prize for second place.

In many spheres of human endeavour, success only arises from demonstrating superiority over one's closest rival. Generals in the armed forces seek every nugget of intelligence about the enemy. They interrogate defectors for any hint of vulnerabilities that can be exploited. One of the most popular management guides in the 1990s was based upon an extended military metaphor. In *The Leadership Secrets of Attila The Hun*, Wess Roberts concludes that "for huns, conflict is a natural state". In warfare, dissecting the capabilities of the enemy is brutal, callous, and unavoidable.

Elsewhere, soccer managers obsess about the strengths and weaknesses of their opponents. They send scouts to watch their rivals in action, and file reports highlighting areas of exposure. They use mind-games to unnerve the other side, or unsettle their players by allowing transfer rumours to fester. A devious and wily manager can be as vital to league success as the calibre of the playing squad.

Business strategists have much to learn from the mindset of leaders in the armed forces and the premier league. Devising products that knock the competition sideways can be a mental and physical ordeal. But the sweat and strife is essential for victory, especially in an era when many markets are stagnant, and revenue growth only arises through stealing share from others. Those who are inattentive to the competition will be overrun. Figuratively, their weapons will be stolen and their villages destroyed.

When the landscape is chaotic, packed with aggressive rival organisations seeking to outdo one another, strategists broadly have two options.

DIFFERENTIATION, OR LOWEST COST PROVISION

Differentiation assumes a premium price is merited for the product or service on offer. The onus lies with the firm to justify sound reasons for potential customers to pay an excess. The reasons may be rational, such as durability, reliability or efficiency. Or they may be emotional, for example brand name reassurance. In either case, the strategist should test that the differentiation is difficult for others to copy, enhance or make redundant.

Lowest cost provision assumes that, regardless of market dynamics, the firm will be able to sustain a price point cheaper than any competitor's. If the firm is a traditional bricks-and-mortar operator, the strategist will be conscious of threats to the low-cost status from online sources and from imports. Customers who saved a nickel by purchasing from Firm B in preference to Firm A are unlikely to feel pangs of conscience when Firm C tempts them to switch by shaving off one nickel more.

In most cases, the choice is stark between a differentiation strategy, and a lowest cost provision strategy. Both paths cannot be navigated simultaneously. The implications are often mutually exclusive, and permeate every corner of the organisation.

A competitive strategy based upon differentiation will require expertise in fields such as marketing, research and development, and service. The culture will be designed to stimulate innovation, flexibility and change. Pay will be generous and working arrangements indulgent. Features will multiply and price points will be piloted as the business seeks to optimise its return on sales. Niche distribution channels will be employed to reach and penetrate obscure segments of the market that place particular value on the products on offer.

A firm choosing the lowest cost route will look very different. In this case, success will depend upon discretionary spend being squeezed without sympathy. Variety will be eliminated so that the firm can focus on delivering a few products in exceptionally high volumes. Average salaries will be lower, with bonuses only granted if the short-term finances stack up. The central skill set will be operational expertise, delivered by engineers or process designers with the nose to eke out every last percentage point of margin.

Either strategy will only be effective if leaders have accurate, timely information on competitor activities. Firms cannot base their strategy on being the lowest cost provider if someone else is persistently undercutting by five per cent. They cannot pursue differentiation if someone else has already completed the land-grab. Many chief executives make it a personal mission to know their competitors' product range as intimately as their own. Benchmarking experts are employed to offer independent assessments of "ours versus theirs" using specified criteria. Investment banks, energy firms and supermarkets are among the obsessive users of benchmarking insights during strategic development activities.

As with commanders taking troops into combat, successful chief executives leverage the spectre of a vicious and deadly enemy to galvanise their teams. Glory, they bellow, can only be savoured when victory over the other side is secure.

BEST PRACTICE IN ACTION

PLANET PHARMACY

Planet Pharmacy operates retail and wholesale centres in the Middle East.

To improve the quality of earnings from their estate, it was essential that in-store practice was always equal or superior to that of rival stores. A visual merchandising programme themed "Fast Forward" sought to make shopping enjoyable for customers, with items easy to locate. This policy was the catalyst for encouraging return visits, a key factor driving long-term growth.

Different strategies were identified for high-end, promotional, staple, low-priced and sale products.

LET'S FLEE THE STATE
08

AVOIDING BLOOPERS:

GOVERNMENT CAN MAKE OR BREAK YOU

- Early strategic planning scholars underestimated government as a market participant

- The apparatus of government extends to quangos, regulators and the third sector

- Incumbents benefit from owning assets such as infrastructure, licenses or trademarks

- Major policy changes are now subject to consultation with business and the wider public

In 1900, government accounted for just 15 per cent of economic activity within the United Kingdom. By 2010, this had risen to 45 per cent. Strategists who fail to consider the implications of this pervasive change do so at their peril.

Even these sizeable figures do insufficient justice to the role of government within modern economies. Already, in sectors providing a social service, such as education or healthcare, government is a direct participant and major employer. But its reach is far broader.

In many commercial spheres, the quantum of supply is inherently limited. Official policy controls the supply of rail services, shopping centre development, and residential housing, since removal of any restrictions would cause environmental degradation and social havoc. Physics affects the supply of broadcasting frequencies, and resource availability affects the supply of coal and oil. In such cases, the role of government is often the award of franchising, planning or licensing contracts to firms that meet documented standards and fulfil the terms of a lengthy and expensive procurement process.

In other areas, the principal issue is not the control of supply but the protection of the consumer interest. As industries were being technically privatised in the 1980s and 1990s, governments were ironically equipping themselves with greater powers to intervene across large swatches of the economy through intrusive regulation. Financial services, gas safety engineering, and food production, all fall within this category. In each case, the nature and terms of regulation are constantly evolving, influenced by lobbying groups that act either in the consumer or trade interest.

Early strategic planning scholars underestimated government as a market participant. They often assumed the central dynamic involved willing customers procuring goods and services from willing sellers on purist free market terms, and overlooked the "biggest kid on the block". Yet many businesses owe their prosperity, sometimes their very existence, to their relationship with government.

The term *government* can sometimes be misleading. Literally, it refers to the few dozen lords and MPs who have been made ministers of the Crown, and are responsible for initiating legislation and overseeing departments of state. However, the apparatus of government is more complex and extensive than this simplistic theory might suggest, and often the greatest influence resides some distance from Westminster. It includes civil servants who have laboured in the same department through successive governments, and are masters at blocking the flow of material into the red boxes. It includes the leaders of quangos and regulators, many of which carry dubious democratic accountability. It even includes charitable organisations, often as reliant on state funding as on shaking collection tins on the high street.

For these reasons, the public sector can be a greater guarantor of a firm's long-term stability than any transitory business partner. While blue-chip corporations rise and fall, it is harder to envisage a dramatic withdrawal of the state's tentacles in the decades ahead.

STRATEGIC ASSETS

John Kay was the first economist to explicitly link the force of government with commercial longevity. In his book The *Foundations of Corporate Success*, he analysed a range of businesses that endured over many decades. His purpose was to identify the factors that make success truly sustainable. During his research, he developed the concept of "strategic assets", meaning that a given firm benefits from owning assets such as infrastructure, licenses or trademarks, especially when it is the incumbent, and when market restrictions exist. He concluded: "A high proportion of European industry is either owned by government, has government as its principal supplier, or operates in a sector in which government action substantially influences both entry and competition."

Powergen was the junior electricity generator created by the break-up and privatisation of the Central Electricity Generating Board in 1991. Yet during the 11 years that preceded its acquisition by E-ON, there was scarcely a corner of its operations that was not subject to government inspection, regulation, control or monitoring.

Attending to public policy matters is an increasingly legitimate role for business to embrace. The term "lobbying" derives from the act of tackling political representatives in hotel lobbies, government office lobbies and even Central Lobby itself – the vaulted chamber connecting the House of Commons with the House of Lords. Major policy changes are now subject to open consultation, with responses posted on government websites regardless of their authorship. It is generally accepted that better law-making results from this type of transparent engagement with interested stakeholders.

At times, government has arguably intervened to the excessive benefit of market leaders with entrenched positions, that employ large workforces and can afford teams of policy lobbyists. In the UK, the balance seems to be shifting. Francis Maude, paymaster general in the Coalition government, described in 2012 the administration's plans for a "big society", where power is pushed into the hands of neighbourhoods and citizens. Much of the growth in private sector employment has recently been driven by small business.

Key players in the big society vision are the so-called social entrepreneurs. These organisations bridge the gap between the public and private sector activity at a local level. They are run on commercial terms, but work alongside public authorities to deliver positive social outcomes. Arguing strongly that more investment needs to be channelled in this direction, Maude writes: "We will do all we can to make it happen."

THE PERSONAL FINANCE SOCIETY

The Personal Finance Society (PFS) is the UK's professional body for financial advisers.

The role of many PFS members is being redefined as a result of the recommendations of the regulator's Retail Distribution Review, currently taking effect. The opening session at the PFS's annual board-led strategy review involves understanding and anticipating the emerging regulatory landscape. As a result, strategic priorities are redefined.

In recent years, these have involved the expansion of the PFS's continuing professional development (CPD) activities, as well as enhancing services for segments of the marketplace, such as paraplanning, which are gaining in stature.

NO BOLDER AND NO BRIGHTER

09

NEW FOR 1908
MODEL T FORD

NEW FOR 1908
FASTER HORSE SHOES

AVOIDING BLOOPERS:
INNOVATE TO SURVIVE

- The product life cycle entails a near-inevitable progression through creation, growth, maturity and decline

- Innovation enables firms to break free from the cycle, and reinvent themselves for the next generation

- The fuse of innovation is lit when managers feel empowered to take risks

- Breakthrough innovation relies upon the art of persuasion as much as the product idea

The characteristics of tap water have remained largely unchanged since sanitary engineering first allowed clean potable water to be piped into homes and businesses during the late nineteenth century. No one expects the basic product to be continually re-engineered, rebadged, rebranded, refined, reinvented or relaunched. (Market leaders in water supply, and one or two similar sectors, may wish to skip this chapter.)

Tap water aside, the overwhelming majority of firms face the alarming inevitability of the Product Life Cycle phenomenon. Using the premise that products, like agriculture, are subject to four seasons, the Life Cycle posits that they must pass through:

The creation stage. Like tiny shoots breaking through the topsoil, the product moves from laboratory to pilot. Its appeal is limited to early adopters purchasing through specialist distribution channels.

The growth stage. Word-of-mouth and positive publicity is the catalyst to broaden the product's customer base. Rising sales volumes generate cashflow that can be redeployed to boost awareness through multi-media advertising, and attract new distributors.

The maturity stage. Mainstream wholesalers stockpile the product; mainstream retailers make premium space available. Across ages, income brackets and ethnicity, consumers in their droves regard the product as a household essential.

The decline stage. Fashion changes, tastes evolve, the public moves on. The product is caught in a spaghetti junction of falling sales, retailer price cuts, and reducing margins. Unchecked, the product stumbles from crisis to crisis, until an axe-wielding executive targets it for extinction.

Innovation is the only way to disrupt the near-fatal progression of this cycle, and strategists should argue for reinvestment as soon as a product enters its maturity stage, before it is too late. Voices will be raised against innovation. Some will proclaim: "If it ain't broke, don't fix it." Others will see mature products as corporate cash cows, "providing the money we need to cover the costs of our less successful stock-keeping units (SKUs)". But, counter-intuitively, it is precisely when sales are booming and customers are lining-up around the block that executives should challenge themselves in the most searching manner.

In their book *Killer Differentiators*, Jacky Tai and Wilson Chew use a taut analytical framework to systematically anatomise and investigate the concept of competitive advantage. Ahead of differentiation strategies such as service, quality and people, they place the ability to innovate, and to associate the firm with "the next generation".

Tai and Chew show how one company, Motorola, has progressively reapplied a core idea since the 1930s in order to commercialise car radios, walkie talkies, lunar communications, mobile phones, pagers and wireless cable modems.

Innovation is far from straightforward. Destruction can be more fun, and is certainly easier, than building something new. It seems almost a rule of nature that large organisations have a compulsive sceptic on the payroll, who mutters scornfully and offers dismissive comments about having "done it all before" and "it will never work".

Organisations that wish to use the power of innovation to reinvent themselves and their products must embrace a culture where managers feel empowered to take calculated risks. 3M has enshrined this ethos in its corporate values, which include the statements: "Tolerance for honest mistakes" and "Thou shalt not kill a new product idea".

CREATING THE NEED

Designing and manufacturing a next generation product needs patience, perseverance and scrupulous focus. But, even then, the job is half-finished. Ivory tower innovation may be a legitimate practice for university research departments, but it can be the death knell in the commercial sector. Private equity firms witness countless breakthrough innovations that fall flat – not because they won't function as a piece of engineering, but due to inadequate communication and persuasion.

The genius of firms such as Apple, Nokia and Oakley is not only their incessant, restless focus on "what's next?". It is also their prowess in expressing new ideas. They display a rare knack for creating messages that capture the imagination of next generation buyers.

No business should rely upon its prospective customers to decipher the practical value of unfamiliar products. No one was clamouring for search engines, or social media sites, or cloud computing, before their invention by Silicon Valley visionaries. Focus groups would not have disclosed a requirement. And the instinct of the average consumer is to stick with what works unless offered a compelling reason to change. The recent biography of Steve Jobs reveals that he spent as much time engrossed with his signature promotional campaigns, and seeking exposure in *Time Magazine* and *Newsweek*, as he did perfecting software, weight and casing.

Virtuoso communication is never more vital than when launching breakthrough products. For compulsive innovators, the *persuasion* challenge is uncertain, complicated, risky …and 100 per cent essential.

BEST PRACTICE IN ACTION

THE CHARITIES AID FOUNDATION

The Charities Aid Foundation (CAF) is a charity that connects donors to causes that matter to them.

It has also been a pioneer in the field of social investment. Its ground-breaking CAF Venturesome brand contains the UK's greatest concentration of expertise able to apply innovative financial arrangements to assist the third sector. With social investment poised for growth, supported by favourable government policy and the emergence of new philanthropists, the incoming director of social investment undertook a strategic review to ensure Venturesome maintains its innovation edge.

The scope of the strategy includes dramatic innovation in both the functioning of social investment (adapting principles such as co-investment and quasi-equity) as well as the measurement and rewarding of social impact.

BUILT TO LAST ...
FOR A BIT
<u>10</u>

AVOIDING BLOOPERS:

SUCCESS MUST BE
SUSTAINABLE

- The value of a customer rises as the relationship endures

- Loyal customers are more likely to refer, upgrade and advocate

- Creating communities and sharing success are cornerstones of long-term loyalty

- The gold standard for firms is loyalty among a wider network of customers, staff, suppliers and investors

- In uncertain times, loyalty is a powerful risk management tool

For a few fleeting days in the summer of 2012, London captivated the world's attention as host for the Olympic Games. I recall standing on the Thames Embankment in the shadow of Big Ben, drenched by the torrential downpour, as the marathon runners raced by. Gone, while the camera's focus was still adjusting. The Westminster section complete, they were hurtling onwards towards the Mall.

Unlike top athletes, too many businesses find themselves running to stand still. No sooner is an achievement in place, than it starts to leak out of the back door. Out of necessity, firms are drawn back to protecting the status quo, rather than progressing to the next landmark.

Frederich Reichheld, author of *The Loyalty Effect*, has studied the damage caused when firms are so distracted by leakage they cannot move forward. He calculates that major corporations can lose half their customers every five years, half their employees every four, and half their investors in less than one. Not only does that mean writing-off much of the investment committed to acquiring these stakeholders; it also means incurring the time, cost and risk of replacing every single one.

Loyalty, in Reichheld's eyes, in the key to sustainability. When firms approach a rate of zero defections, then every new customer becomes accretive.

Some leaders see customer retention as an operational matter, and disregard the loyalty effect when strategic options are considered. Yet the financial consequences of customer loyalty are startling. Across many sectors, economic studies demonstrate that the annual profit from a given customer steadily rises as the relationship extends over time. Servicing costs reduce since customers are familiar with features. Loyal customers are less likely to complain. They purchase ancillary products and services. They enthusiastically upgrade to a higher price point. The combined impact is that profit per customer can rise, every year, for at least seven years after the point of first contact, before stabilising. For this reason, loyalty is a powerful filter strategists can use to assess ideas for future development. Strategies that bind people closer to the organisation must be treasured and nourished.

Referrals are the cherished by-product of loyalty. When prospective purchasers survey a market, they quickly encounter the aggrandising claims corporations make about themselves, and are understandably sceptical. But they give credence to the opinions of anyone untainted by vested interest.

So, when their customers undergo a metamorphosis into advocates, compulsively extolling a product's benefits, firms can be breathe more easily. When customers offer to provide a personal demonstration of the product to their family, friends, colleagues and peers, with all the gusto of a commissioned salesforce, firms can be justifiably proud.

TWO CORNERSTONES

Conscious of these issues, the strategist should ensure the two cornerstones of long-term loyalty are dug deep.

Community creation. Customers who harbour a sense of belonging and kinship are unlikely to defect. There is an affiliation between football supporters and their chosen club that is almost unbreakable – men are more likely to divorce than change their sporting allegiances. Loyalty to the community defies logic. Rationally, it is absurd to stick with a team that has endured relegation, offloaded its star players, and lost its manager to its closest rival (a fate suffered, for example, by Birmingham City Football Club in 2011 within six months of their historic Carling Cup triumph). Why not switch support to a big brand name? Football clubs nurture a passion that provides a buffer against hard times, the same aura that is seen amongst devotees of legendary rock bands, or zealous participants at a Star Trek convention.

Success sharing. Recognising the economic value of loyalty, some firms are willing to share this benefit with their customers. Supermarkets offer loyalty points that can be redeemed for cash vouchers; airlines offer free flights; hotels offer upgrades. These are differing tactics but they work towards the common goal of providing existing customers with concrete reasons to stick around.

Customer loyalty is to be relished. But the gold standard is loyalty among the wider network of staff, suppliers and investors. The successful firm builds a series of cooperative structures, where all parties benefit from their status as insiders, and are penalised if they behave opportunistically. Sociologist Geert Hofstede observes that eastern societies are culturally amenable to the sharing of value, underpinned by their long-term orientation. From South Korea to Japan, firms proliferate in clusters, trading with each other in materials, knowledge and vision, to the benefit of the entire network. By contrast, the west relies more upon immediate gratification.

In today's globalised economy, more western organisations are adopting the best practices they detect in other cultures. They are finding the loyalty of a network is an outstanding risk management tool. In uncertain times, there are many "what if?" scenarios that could cause widespread disruption. What if the economy goes into freefall? What if the euro collapses? What if our competitors double their marketing spend? What if we receive bad press? What if we suffer a systemic service failure? What expensive contingencies need to be developed?

If stakeholders are fickle enough to defect during a short-term crisis, or in retaliation to any temporary misfortune, then a company's existence can be imperilled. Loyalty creates a sturdy bulwark against such a dangerous outcome. There is no reason for any firm meekly to accept such a risk.

BEST PRACTICE IN ACTION

PPP HEALTHCARE

PPP healthcare is a leading private healthcare insurer.

A large segment of its market involves corporate buyers who, in the increasingly competitive late 1990s, were switching to rival providers on a whim. PPP sought compelling reasons to justify loyalty and long-term partnership, and executed this through the development of ancillary services. The acquisition and integration of a firm offering sickness and absence management services proved to be a vital initiative.

PPP successfully began to reposition itself from simply writing out insurance cheques after the event, to actively engaging with healthcare issues from the moment symptoms first become apparent.

BUSY FOOLS

11

SET PRIORITIES

- Strategies should not be shopping lists, let alone wish lists

- The setting of priorities can be informed by analysing business units as cash cows, stars, dogs or question marks

- Setting priorities requires confidence, discipline, focus and collective responsibility

- Effective priorities should be both desirable and achievable

"**A** n astronaut, an inventor, a footballer and an actor," replied one of my sons, when asked to describe his perfect career. This scatterbrain response is not, of course, confined to pre-teens. It characterises at least half the strategic plans one ever reads.

Strategies should not be shopping lists, let alone wish lists. Endless pages portraying an Aladdin's cave of projects, programmes, feasibility studies and reviews do not amount to a strategy. They will confuse readers, and – even worse – leave those tasked with implementation feeling bewildered and rudderless. Such a strategy has failed to reach the first base of giving common purpose and direction.

The chief executive of *AXA UK* once said, "We are fundamentally a lazy organisation." With this typically eye-catching turn of phrase, he was making a serious and profound point. Successful firms, he was arguing, concentrate on a limited number of things. One of AXA's most consummate attributes was, and remains, its ability to select those priorities.

Composing a two-page strategic plan can be far harder than writing one that rambles for a hundred pages or more, because setting priorities is not straightforward. It requires confidence, discipline and focus. Placing a few bets, not spreading one's hunches wildly, is only viable for punters that have studied the form and understand the odds.

Businesses that are skilled at prioritisation possess a formidable degree of insight into the opportunities and threats that lie beyond the horizon. Retrospectively, it can be clear there were two or three turning-points that made the difference between success and failure. Moving into Brazil just as the economy was liberalising; shutting down a product line the moment the technology was becoming obsolete. But, without the benefit of hindsight, how can these bets be confidently placed?

MARKET SHARE AND GROWTH

In many organisations, a popular tool to inform priority-setting is the Boston Box, also known as the BCG (Boston Consulting Group) Portfolio, or the Growth-Share Matrix. The Box involves two axes – one concerned with the external marketplace (quantifying the anticipated growth rate on a scale), and the other with the company's own market position (quantifying the market share relative to the leader). The analysis allows each product or service line within a firm's portfolio to be placed into one of the four quadrants created by the axes:

Stars (high market growth, high market share). The sector is expanding rapidly, and the business unit is likely to be cash generative. Nevertheless, it justifies further investment, beyond its generation capability, to secure its long-term position and ensure opportunities are fully realised. Verdict: Prioritise for investment.

Dogs (low market growth, low market share). The business unit has a poor competitive position, and cash is being absorbed in perpetuity with no realistic prospect of achieving commercial viability. Verdict: Deprioritise – ideally divest, otherwise scale down.

Cash cows (low market growth, high market share). The business unit has a strong, entrenched position, and enjoys healthy cashflow. Scale means unit costs are low relative to the sector. However, competitors may be engaging in target practice, and the market leader is the likely bullseye. Complacency can lead to ruin. Verdict: Some prioritisation – sufficient to maintain current standing and deter rivals.

Question marks (high market growth, low market share). An opportunity has been identified, but success is uncertain. The business unit lacks a cash generation capability, and requires speculative investment if the potential is to be realised. Verdict: The status quo is untenable – prioritise or shut down. The final choice will depend upon the number of other opportunities within the portfolio, the firm's overall risk appetite, and its ability to access financing.

Where companies get the big decisions right, the fate of all the second-tier suggestions becomes immaterial. My paper, *A Winning Approach to Strategic Business Planning*, gives a number of case studies of firms that made well-judged big decisions, securing and leveraging a strong market position.

The entry of *Stakis Hotels* into the nursing home sector was one such example. Three priorities were agreed. The first was to identify locations with favourable local metrics, including demographics (age and wealth distribution), and the quantity and nature of existing supply. The second was to create a national brand identity, Ashbourne Homes, so the company's name would be recognised as a mark of quality and integrity to families during a distressing time. The third was to operate a suite of high-margin services, sufficiently flexible so that the care solution could be tailored according to the different levels of price sensitivity within the customer base. In the strategic plan, these three ideas were elevated and resourced above all else. They enabled the successful divestment of the business unit once critical mass was achieved.

The trick, of course, is that corporations do not have the luxury of hindsight, and there will be differing opinions around the board table about where the priorities lie. This should not deter strategists from the process. It might be easier in the short-run to placate the board by giving equal time in the plan to everybody's pet project. It would also be a monumental error. Instead, the range of views in the room should be used constructively, to generate an even better end-result. Objective challenge, debate and rebuttal can be used to suppress the weaker ideas, and ensure the strongest priorities are endorsed and resourced.

Effective priorities should be both desirable and achievable. The strategic plan must make clear that executive sponsorship is unstinting, and that support will be forthcoming to tackle obstacles as they arise. Nay saying or backsliding should be vigorously resisted. The leaders of outstanding organisations are equally likely to display collective responsibility towards agreed priorities as the men and women who comprise the British Cabinet (perhaps more so).

BEST PRACTICE IN ACTION

THE CHARTERED INSTITUTE OF PURCHASING AND SUPPLY

The Chartered Institute of Purchasing and Supply is the professional body for the procurement sector.

The board and management team decided its stakeholders would best be served by identifying a discrete set of strategic priorities that would be the focus for the majority of time, energy and investment. These were: brand, international, leadership, technology and the profile of the profession.

Board reports were streamlined to show progress against specified milestones for each one of these five priorities.

WE DON'T DO ACTION
12

UNDERSTAND HOW TO GET THERE

- "A bias for action" must be more powerful than the forces of inertia

- A causal relationship should exist between actions and results

- Effective implementation demands clarity around actions, responsibilities, resourcing, dependencies and dates

- Employment and remuneration practices should recognise honest strivers who display a commitment to deliver

Legend has it that the attics of North America are straining under the weight of cases packed with unread copies of the *National Geographic* magazine. Unfortunately, the same observation can be made about the fate of too many perfectly-formed strategic plans. Full-day workshops are held for managers to pore over the finer points of drafting. The finished product is launched with panache, speeches, and canapés. But then the active life of the plan is over in precious moments, as it completes the short journey from the local print shop to the top shelf of managers' darkened cupboards.

Peters and Waterman, in *In Search of Excellence*, describe "a bias for action" as one vital ingredient within America's most successful corporations. Yet, in many large organisations, the forces of inertia are more powerful than the impulse for change and action. Managers earning decent salaries and with enviable job security look with concern at strategies that upset the comfort of their "known knowns". Those whose inadequacies may be exposed by a new direction can vastly outnumber the potential beneficiaries. Inevitably, such people are also in the prime positions to block and thwart.

Chapters 3 and 4 spoke of the value of understanding "where we are" and "where we want to be". But this exercise turns to dust if little attention is paid to the third and final leg: "how to get there". Action plans, argue Peters and Waterman, mean that strategy becomes more than forlorn hope.

Getting there is about crossing the bridge between the current and future states, a bridge that is built in the right direction, connecting with the other side. In many plans, it is possible to read the vision, and then turn to the action list, and find almost no connection. Every action could be executed sublimely, on time and to specification, yet the organisation would be no closer to its goals. Occasionally, actions even describe a journey heading in the diametrically opposed direction.

The strategist must create a causal relationship between actions and results, between inputs and outputs.

If connections cannot be traced *back* from results to actions, they are wishful thinking. So, if a key strategy is to create a customer experience fit for the twenty-first century, does the plan hint at the actions necessary to make it happen?

If connections cannot be drawn *forward* from actions to results, then the action should be removed from the plan, since time is being wasted on projects which are not mission critical. For example, if the main action is opening a Frankfurt office while the strategy is expanding into Africa, a disconnect has arisen between action and strategy that must be resolved.

SIX ELEMENTS

The starting pistol for implementing an action plan can be fired when six key elements are in place.

Actions must be drafted precisely, without ambiguity. And, being actions, a verb can often be illuminating! An action such as "Budapest market entry" misses the one word that would clarify what is actually intended. "Evaluate", "prepare for", "deliver", "review" and "stop" would each place a very different spin on the strategist's intentions.

A named individual must be shown as accountable for delivery. If too many names are listed against an action, or if there are none at all, the upshot is identical; nobody feels in charge, so the likelihood of progress is remote. A whole team of technicians and runners may be asked to support the leader, but the focus of ultimate responsibility should not be blurred.

Required resources must be estimated and made available. Resource mapping is relevant both at the level of an individual project, and for those with a wider purview. In many organisations, the pool of able and willing volunteers is limited, and these individuals are nominated repeatedly. Encouraging talented people to stretch themselves is crucial in the development of tomorrow's leaders. Over-stretch and burn-out benefit no one.

Dependencies must be identified and managed. Where key actions cannot commence until other actions are complete, strategists must be alert to dependencies. A delay in, for example, a systems release will have repercussions for the marketing campaign that relies upon it. Where chain reactions could arise, additional resources may need to be marshalled to safeguard momentum.

Key dates must be shown, either in the form of calendar dates or elapsed time from project commencement. Actions should be given start dates and end dates, and the major milestones identified. These should then be cross-matched against other timelines. For example, it may be unwise to coincide a network overhaul with the busiest time of the year for customer bookings.

The sixth element cannot be found in any project management software package, but it is the stardust that turns entries on a GANNT chart (named after the mechanical engineer and management consultant Henry Gannt) into real commitment. Senior managers must foster a culture where *commitment to deliver* is rewarded, not deterred. Honest strivers who have fallen short should not be penalised while bonuses are lavished on those who have been relaxing and pontificating on the sidelines.

This scenario, far from rare in corporate Britain, scatters toxic fallout across a firm. Rare but brave is the organisation that promotes the person who, having been behind the wheel for an almighty car-crash, has learnt valuable and salient lessons that can be used to great advantage.

BEST PRACTICE IN ACTION

NETCARE

Netcare is South Africa's leading healthcare group with extensive operations in the United Kingdom.

Many parts of its service involve bidding for, and then mobilising for, complex long-term contracts. Netcare's culture is built around personal responsibility and reliability.

Regardless of the size of the assignment, bid stages and mobilisation stages are led by named project managers, with significant devolved authority, who are tasked to get the job done on time and to specification. Weekly flash reports, and detailed reports as major milestones approach, are enshrined as working practices.

As a result, the organisation avoids sudden surprises that can undermine trust and derail momentum.

CHAOS THEORY
13

AVOIDING BLOOPERS:
GET YOUR TEAMS ALIGNED

- Poor alignment can arise from geographically dispersed units doing their own thing

- It also originates when departments start to operate maverick mini-plans

- Alignment is possible when leaders focus upon big issues, leaving local problem-solving to management judgement

- Training, incentives and celebrations all reinforce tightness of fit around core principles

Complex bureaucratic organisations are a curious phenomenon that, after thousands of years, only emerged in the past two centuries as the dominant vehicle for managing trading relationships. Human evolution has yet to catch up. Managers are still acquiring the skills and capabilities the corporate beast demands. They instinctively resist tasks that have been mandated by anonymous paper-pushers elsewhere in the company food chain. They mutter, defy and thwart. That is why getting teams aligned can seem so thankless.

An unwritten clause in the job description of most chief executives is that, in between investor calls and board meetings, endless hours must be dedicated to resolving heated disputes between factions, behaving like Doctor Doolittle's notorious pushmi-pullyu creature; one body with two brains, each promoting a contradictory view of the direction to be trod.

Poor alignment within organisations can take two forms. Firstly, *geographically dispersed units* may each be doing their own thing. Outposts may have been acquired, but not assimilated, with management and staff resisting the imposition of alien processes and methodologies. They point to the success they enjoyed when they were independent as evidence that global corporate policies are ill-advised. They argue that local market conditions are unique – specific customs and practices are embedded, a patchwork of local regulations are in force, the unwary can incur inadvertent tax liabilities. Such factors, they stress, mean firms must be sensitive to local market conditions, the very antithesis of the "think group act group" head office mindset.

Secondly, *functions around the firm* may be operating maverick mini-plans, regardless of the wider picture. The corporate strategy may demand white-hot growth, yet the finance department may be in hunkering-down mode. The corporate strategy may assume expansion into emerging countries, yet the technology department may be preoccupied with imposing standardisation in existing territories. The corporate strategy may be to shift gears upmarket, yet the sales department may be heavily discounting into mass distribution channels. Each one of these strategies can be legitimate in certain circumstances. What makes no sense is when one half of the business has adopted plans that are, prima facia, incompatible with those being pursued by the other half.

When the early 1990s recession hit, cruise operator *Cunard Line* recognised it faced a problem. Revenues plummeted as holiday makers forsook the annual vacation, and even high rollers opted for cheaper staterooms. Yet it took a concerted effort to secure alignment around a consistent response. The marketing plan assumed operational spend would take the hit: after all, with high fixed costs, every additional passenger, however steep the discount, made a contribution to overheads. The operational plan assumed marketing spend would be slashed, so as not to alienate the loyal customers who were at least providing some income. Only when these documents were fused into a whole did it become apparent that a misalignment between two worldviews needed to be addressed.

How then to reconcile the firm's need for alignment with the human impulse for freedom? Is there a balance between consistency and anarchy?

WINNING HEARTS AND MINDS

In *Built to Last*, Jim Collins and Jerry Porras suggest that managers must be allowed to "experiment, change, adapt". Organisations which are highly prescriptive about the small stuff struggle to attract high calibre individuals able to use judgement and experience to solve problems.

But, they continue, initiative is only practical when there is "cult-like" tightness around a core ideology, around key principles, around the big issues that flag on the radar of customers and investors. The strategic plan must concern itself with these themes. If it gets immersed into the microcosm of operational detail, it will fail.

Collins and Porras discuss three companies that get the big things right (Nordstrom, Proctor and Gamble, and Disney), and list some of the tangible mechanisms they employ to achieve alignment. Some are self-evident: training, incentives that fit the strategy, recognition, awards and celebrations that reinforce success. Others are slightly more outlandish: unique terminology and language, corporate songs and pledges, a mythology around the firm's "heroic deeds", marble statues of corporate luminaries. But, argue the authors, *they work*. And there are numerous examples of behaviours which seem preposterous or idiosyncratic when introduced (recall the outrage when a handful of employers tentatively suggested that smoking might be banned in their offices), but are accepted practices a generation later.

For winning strategists, the big themes are equivalent to the rules of physics. The law of gravity is constant, whether it is observed at a universal, planetary, atomic or sub-atomic level. Similarly, strategy should transcend geography, function, product line or customer segment.

If pockets of the business are undermining key strategies, there will be contagion. Customers will notice misalignment and grow confused. What does the firm stand for? Where is it headed? With remorseless concentration on big themes, organisations have at least a fighting chance of avoiding chaos.

The behaviour of business unit leaders reveals whether an organisation has judged a fine balance between alignment and looseness. It is shown in the attitudes of country managers from Buenos Aires to Berlin to Bangalore – when they not only verbally support the strategy, not only circulate the documents, and not only showcase compliant activity – but spur their teams to figure out what *else* they need to do, off their own initiative, to be a more integral part of the whole.

BEST PRACTICE IN ACTION

CBRE

CBRE is the world's largest professional advisory firm specialising in commercial property.

Across Europe, the Middle East and Africa (EMEA), the firm is present in 43 countries, with 150 offices. With international investors and occupiers increasingly seeking the reassurance of consistent service delivery, CBRE faced the challenge of how best to coordinate activities across timezones, borders and cultures. A series of cross-border groups have been formed, specialising in the range of real estate disciplines such as brokerage, valuation, investment, consultancy, property management, and retail. Each group is headed by a senior CBRE executive, supported by representatives from all major markets.

The groups are charged with creating ever-closer cross-border union. In many cases, internal conferences are now hosted once or twice every year to agree how processes, practices and technologies will be consistently deployed to deliver the same recognisable end-product regardless of where the work is undertaken.

TELEPATHY WORKS (IN SCI-FI)
14

AVOIDING BLOOPERS:
COMMUNICATE BROADLY, DEEPLY AND OFTEN

- Poor communication is a leading cause of frustration for staff within complex organisations

- Communication should reveal how the corporate strategy is relevant to employees' careers and roles

- Both old and new media should be deployed as firms seek the best mix of channels to leverage

- Face-to-face communication, ideally interactive, helps secure buy-in

Politicians are told by their media advisers to be quietly satisfied when they are bored to despair from repeating their policies through interminable interviews. Only when they are exasperated at hearing themselves yet again articulating the same point then, just possibly, might it start seeping into the wider public consciousness.

Similarly, strategists who have been preoccupied with the minutiae of the analytical and developmental process can forget that others do not share their intimate acquaintance with the conclusions. Strategic objectives will not ooze through the layers of the organisation, propelled by a type of corporate osmosis, to those outside the loop. Telepathy can be a useful tool in science fiction storylines, but it has no place in the real world of work.

Communication must be incessant to be effective. In modern life, it is almost impossible to count the messages that assail people every day. Before even setting foot at work, a member of staff may have rolled out from under Versace sheets, squeezed Colgate toothpaste onto an Oral B brush, shouted at the kids to change out of their Spongebob pyjamas, shovelled down Kelloggs corn flakes, jumped into a Paul Smith suit and Churches brogues, checked Facebook, caught the Sky News headlines, and seen a dozen billboard posters while driving an Audi convertible into the central business district. These are just the stirrings of the day's tsunami of messages. Internal communication cannot be half-hearted if it wishes to be heard above the crashing waves.

Employee surveys are often used to obtain 360 degree feedback on facets of corporate culture. They give staff the chance to vent about pay-and-rations, working conditions, management style, or social activities. Regardless of sector or firm size, it is remarkable how often the leading complaint is "they don't tell us what's going on". In some cases, the root cause may be management paranoia about strategies leaking to competitors. In other cases, the problem may be apathy or lack of time. The consequence is the same: frustrated staff, less able to make the contribution expected of them.

For motivational author and speaker Stephen Covey, "empathic communication" is one of the seven habits of highly effective people. It requires investment that, in the short term, managers may see as discretionary. Yet Covey contends that communicating broadly, deeply and often delivers a tremendous and rapid payback. Staff feel bound to the strategy, understand how to participate, and uncover new ways to bring it to life. Organisations which place great importance on internal communications do not simply relay the high-level bullet points. They make it relevant to the lives and roles of their workforce – addressing "what it means to you", "how your role contributes", "actions you can take to bring it closer to fruition".

CHANNELS GALORE

The array of channels used to disseminate strategic messages varies, even among model organisations. The basics have always included staff newsletters, posters and bulletin boards. Since the 1990s, these have been supplemented by email alerts, intranet sites and podcasts. And internal communications teams know a captive audience is an attentive audience, which is why advertising in petrol forecourts is so effective (three minutes, ensnared, until the tank is filled). The office equivalent includes screensavers, which dominate the field of vision while applications are firing up; the back of the elevator (no one likes to start a conversation as it wheezes from floor to floor); and the wall by the coffee machine or microwave (especially in firms where staff habitually queue).

But communicating the strategy to staff cannot rely on old (paper-based) and new (technological) media. In small and medium-sized firms, the chief executive should assume direct responsibility for communicating strategy, providing regular updates to groups of employees during, for example, breakfast briefings and staff forums. In larger firms, such activity may be supplemented by a programme of "cascades", whereby the headlines of the strategy pass from tier to tier through team briefings. In traditional organisations, a member of the leadership team may stand at a lectern delivering a tightly-scripted pep talk accompanied by a slideshow. In others, the format may involve a panel of senior executives in a town hall-style setting, chatting informally in response to prompts from a moderator. Regardless of size or culture, one principle stands. A significant element of staff communication must be face-to-face.

The final groundrule is to make transmission of the strategy as interactive as possible.

Within new media, Web 2.0 technologies have opened up possibilities for staff to engage in asking questions, seeking clarification or posting comments through accessing social networking and blogging sites with restricted internal use. The face-to-face sessions should also encourage participation. For staff, the experience should never be akin to visiting the theatre, sitting passively, being entertained, clapping in appreciation, and then vacating the premises as soon as the curtain calls are concluded. At a minimum, time should be set aside for questions: in fact, many organisations place more value on the Q&A session than the opening plenary remarks.

Many firms go a step further. After the formalities and introductory comments, they ask staff to breakout into small groups of perhaps eight or ten, sitting in circles or around a table. Each team is asked to discuss what they have just heard – raising issues, suggesting implementation ideas, consolidating their feedback through a nominated spokesperson who relays the comments when the meeting reconvenes. There is a gulf between lukewarm acquaintance with the strategy, and full-blooded buy-in. The mark of an outstanding internal communication programme is when the staff body, from boardroom to janitor, are unapologetically squatting in second camp.

SESAME BANKHALL GROUP

Sesame Bankhall Group is the largest distributor of financial advice services in the UK.

In 2003, Sesame was created from the merger of five pre-existing firms under one new brand. Such an ambitious programme of change carried many benefits, but also risks.

For Sesame, the number one short-term task on rebrand day was to ensure staff related to the strategy on many levels: knowing key facts, understanding the significance of the change, applying it to their own roles, and creating new spin-off opportunities. Team leaders were provided with a portfolio of briefing materials, to be used in staggered sessions throughout the morning. Formal team communications were supplemented with competitions, quizzes, live music and entertainment.

Overnight, a special edition of the staff magazine *Open* was published, packed with photographs and comments from rebrand day under the heading "Thanks for the memory".

THE GHOST OF UNCLE JOE
15

BE FLEXIBLE; IT WORKS FOR ENTREPRENEURS

- Fixed five year plans failed in the USSR; decades later, the world still awaits a leader who can make them viable

- Too often, the prevailing attitude is: "It was in the plan; it must be done"

- Many of the greatest business breakthroughs are rooted in opportunism

- The entrepreneurial instinct is to use highly-sensitive antennae to adapt quickly

During his rule of the Soviet Union, Joseph Stalin used the concept of a Five-Year Plan to devastating, and ultimately futile, effect.

Seated in the Kremlin, he issued instructions about the annual improvements that would be achieved in every aspect of Soviet society, from military preparations to Siberian factories. Equally evil and delusional, nothing was left to the discretion of local managers. He believed that, simply by issuing a central edict, output would advance remorselessly, exponentially, for years to come. It took the collapse of the Soviet Empire for the truth to emerge, and the world to see the tragic, horrendous chasm between Stalin's edicts and the facts on-the-ground.

Fixed five year plans failed in the USSR; decades later, the world still awaits a leader who can make them viable. And until such time, strategies need to be dynamic and evolving, not static and untouchable.

Although they are rarely of such geo-political significance, five year plans imposed by corporate chief executives upon their organisations have the same disconnect with reality. Even worse, is when the chief executive expects blind allegiance to the rigidities of the plan, and a prevailing acceptance that: "It was in the plan; it must be done". This is not a prescription for adroit, dynamic delivery. The default position of managers should not be to close their eyes, and soldier on regardless.

A five year *vision* is admirable. In fact, for entrepreneurs, it is arguably their most indispensable asset. Firms do not become world-beaters without a vision that can stay the course. Travelling along the Silk Route through Uzbekistan, one might decide that a taxi beats a train for the leg out of Bukhara, but China remains the destination. The trick for business is to use short-term opportunism to speed progress towards (and not get distracted from) the agreed goals.

Rigid plans are hardly worth a candle. Days into the delivery of any plan, strategists should be adapting tactics in light of market signals. If a new product has been launched, what early feedback is being received from retailers? Does the customer promise need to be fine-tuned? Should elements of the marketing strategy be reshuffled? If an assertive competitor parks their proverbial tanks on one's lawn, what options are available and how might the scenario play out?

In each case, the strategist's instinct is to behave nimbly and flexibly, not bound to fulfil a schedule of tasks that may have been determined under very different circumstances.

Successful entrepreneurs adapt quickly, responding to information received via their highly-sensitive antennae. They achieve breakthroughs through blatant, unapologetic opportunism.

James Dyson has been one of Britain's most formidable innovators over the past 20 years, building a reported personal net worth of £1.6 billion. His autobiography, *Against The Odds*, is a 280-page paean to the virtues of opportunism. His first invention was, in fact, nothing to do with the dual cyclone bagless vacuum cleaners for which he ultimately became famous. It was a reimagined wheelbarrow, called a ballbarrow.

Had Dyson adhered blindly to the ballbarrow plan, he would have either changed the nature of gardening forever, or receded into obscurity. Instead, his restless imagination chanced upon an idea with more breath-taking potential. At this point, he had no hesitation. He shelved the ballbarrow plan, and changed course.

His recounting of the next few years is a tale of opportunistic dodging and weaving. Experience bought new insights into the shortcomings of traditional vacuum cleaners, how consumers chose to use a Dyson cleaner (which varied widely by culture), and the pros and cons of controlling distribution. Plans were reset to reflect his greater knowledge; the business model evolved to suit new circumstances. At every turn, flexibility won over blind subservience to facts that had become irrelevant.

SKUNKWORKS AND INCUBATORS

Inertia is often hard-wired into the DNA of large businesses. With the average sales of a top 250 US corporation being over $10 bn, a large proportion of industry now resembles the proverbial oil tanker (ponderous and lumbering when asked to change direction) rather than a speedboat. Recognising that the merits of flexibility cannot be entirely foregone, successive attempts have been made to combine the firepower of the billion dollar balance sheet with the agility of a start-up.

Lockheed pioneered the skunkwords model: an internal project team working with a high degree of autonomy, unhampered by bureaucracy, with key staff seconded from the core business. The less than appetising nomenclature arose because an early skunkworks project was located in WW2 near a plastics factory, reminiscent of the foul-smelling skunkworks factory in Al Capp's Li'l Abner comic strip. A similar model with the same intent has been business incubation parks, occasionally used by large organisations, including NASA, to provide a nurturing environment for start-ups with whom some type of symbiotic and mutually-beneficial relationship can be enjoyed.

An untouchable plan is an undeliverable plan. One that allows for short-term manoeuvring may dazzle. To paraphrase the famous words of *Inc Magazine*, a dynamic plan is the "key to being fast, mobile and opportunistic … the very things entrepreneurs cherish most."

BEST PRACTICE IN ACTION

BRAND JOURNEY VENTURING

Brand Journey Venturing (BJV) is a team of entrepreneurs based in the United States that helps large consumer product businesses to take ideas to revenue within 12 months.

They offer a unique blend of expertise, including strategy and financing, technology and new media, branding and marketing, supply chain management and operations. This combination enables them to deliver outsourced solutions to large firms that are unable, for many reasons, to incubate innovative business concepts effectively. BJV undertakes an appraisal of the proposition, and then – subject to meeting the test of commercial viability – will form the business, develop the product, bring it to market, and nurture it through to critical mass.

As outsourced venturers, the entrepreneurs can respond nimbly to market feedback, refining both product and distribution until the proposition is perfectly pitched for early adopters. Once the venture achieves a steady state, it is returned on pre-agreed terms to the client to further develop.

ON TRACK. I THINK, AT A GUESS, PERHAPS

16

MEASURE YOUR PROGRESS

- Monitoring progress according to a hierarchy of measures enables leaders to remain in control

- The four most valuable measurement categories include financial, customer, internal-business-process and learning and growth

- Progress should be balanced between each category, and between lead and lag indicators

- Successful organisations often use a flash report, or dashboard, to track and monitor high-level progress

eaders have a choice when it comes to the implementation of strategy. They can trust to luck, goodwill and a following wind. Or they can remain in control. In multi-tiered organisations, control depends upon accurate, timely, forward-looking and relevant information. So that's where the problems begin.

The key word in the preceding paragraph was "information": meaning material than *informs*. Many managers confuse information with data. Executives are submerged beneath a virtual deluge of facts, which churns noisily from the office printer as megabytes of email attachments are downloaded in every conceivable format. Data overload may result from back-covering by subordinates, or from deliberate obfuscation. The result will be the same: managers who are unable to manage effectively. Leaders should identify the hierarchy of measures they will use to monitor progress towards strategic objectives; prune them; prune them again; and embed them into processes and behaviours.

THE BALANCED SCORECARD

In *The Balanced Scorecard*, performance experts Robert Kaplan and David Norton suggest that the mix of key indicators available to senior executives should cover four bases.

Financial Perspective: This includes revenue growth and mix, cost reduction and productivity improvement, asset utilisation.

Customer Perspective: This includes market share, customer acquisition, customer retention, customer satisfaction, customer profitability.

Internal-Business-Process Perspective: This includes innovation, operations, post-sale service.

Learning and Growth: This includes employee satisfaction, employee retention, employee productivity, staff competencies, technology infrastructure.

The first principle of the scorecard is to maintain a balance between the firm's progress in each of the four categories. One area should not absorb a disproportionate amount of attention, over-running all others.

The second principle is to maintain a balance between lead and lag indicators. Firms that are single-mindedly preoccupied with tomorrow will not learn the lessons of experience. Firms that are capable only of retrospective analysis will find the future to be a foreign land. Again, the scorecard forces a balance.

Kaplan and Norton's thesis is that balanced organisations are more successful. Excessive focus on, for example, the financial indicators can lead to distorted priorities and counter-productive activity. Firms may be tempted to slash generous customer support programmes. Because there is a lag effect upon customer satisfaction, the immediate profit margins look healthy. But problems are stored up for the years ahead. Similarly, too much attention to internal business processes, rather than learning and growth, can result in a highly efficient operation which lacks the human intervention skills to capitalise. The verdict is that maintaining a deliberate balance means the measures are mutually reinforcing. Over-performing on one, at the expense of the others, becomes destructive.

Within the four categories, indicators must be selected that are strategically meaningful. Some organisations are run using measures that, while beyond reproach when viewed in isolation, bear no relationship to the priorities articulated in the strategic plan. Once again, this can be symptomatic of internal disconnect – for example, between a chief executive in charge of vision, and a finance director concentrating on the current year bottom line.

The accurate reporting of performance against the measures should go without saying. But it can be fiendishly complex. New strategies may require measures that are not yet embedded within computer systems. Programmes need to be written to assist collection, collation and analysis. More troublesome, some strategies may not be empirically measurable, and may instead be subject to judgement and perception. For example, moving into an overseas territory, the strategy may depend upon establishing trusted relationships with local officials. The board may feel it is important to monitor the strength of such relationships, but knows that they cannot be objectively rated like a sales quota. The most accurate source may be the qualitative perception of the local project leader, who will be judging body language, eye contact, and what is both said and unsaid. It may take months before the reliability of these impressions becomes clear.

Once the measures are agreed, successful organisations often use a dashboard, or flash report, to track high-level progress. Traffic light colour coding is typically used to indicate status: green meaning on-track, amber meaning issues are arising but being addressed, and red meaning off-track with a high risk that objectives will be missed. Gradations can be used to show intermediate states, although there is a purity and simplicity to the red-amber-green model that prevents line managers hiding behind nuance and sophistry.

Firms that are committed to ambitious and rapid delivery need to take these indicators seriously. Best practice might involve the chief executive, flanked by his strategist and performance guru, holding progress meetings with the rest of the executive team. Shining a torch upon areas of concern, and drilling into detail where redress might be required, these meetings create the basis for holding managers to account. The more squirming around the table, the more penetrating has been the glare from the chief executive's spotlight.

Being a one-legged duck is incompatible with swimming in a straight line. And unfiltered, poor quality data is incompatible with strategic progress. It is no friend to the winning strategist.

BEST PRACTICE IN ACTION

HEARING AND MOBILITY

Hearing and Mobility offers aids and equipment to help elderly and disabled customers retain an active, independent life, through a chain of retail units.

A priority for the incoming chief executive was to increase the statistical basis for management decisions. Tools were introduced to enable the analysis of sales by product line, and by store, on a weekly, monthly and annual basis. This enabled benchmarking to be conducted in real-time, and searching questions posed when individual units were at odds with the wider picture.

At a strategic level, management could now expedite new product development through piloting, testing and ramping-up.

IT STARTS NEXT MONTH 17

AVOIDING BLOOPERS:
DO IT, IN POWER TIME

- The arch enemy of great strategy is the alluring temptation of procrastination

- Team members should be assigned tasks that match their preferred cognitive level, from remembering to creating

- Power Time applies when exceptional results need to be delivered to aggressive timescales

- Using the six steps of the G-Force method, leaders can inspire their teams to outperformance

No strategy has ever achieved results without human beings making it happen. So, the final enemy of great strategy is the alluring temptation of procrastination, that scourge of modern business.

The first axiom in making it happen is to appreciate the capabilities at one's disposal, and to match individuals with tasks for which they are well-suited. Team members who are asked to bring the force of their skills to progress an issue will respond positively; those who feel intimidated by the task may worry; and those who believe their talents are being overlooked will sulk.

At a 1948 Convention of the American Psychology Association, experts under the leadership of Benjamin Bloom proposed six cognitive levels which are now widely referred to as Bloom's Taxonomy:

Remembering: Showing technical knowledge of the strategy.
Understanding: Appreciating the strategy's essential points.
Applying: Thinking through practical uses of the strategy in new and existing situations.
Analysing: Delving into the breadth and depth of material underlying the strategy.
Judging: Making strategic decisions that require evaluation and assessment.
Creating: Designing solutions by synthesising, rearranging and formulating.

During strategy implementation, *teamwork* involves the judicious synthesis of all six levels. But within teams, there will be *individuals* who are only comfortable operating at certain levels of the taxonomy. When duties within a programme are allocated with sensitivity, team members will be eager to get on with the tasks at hand. If not, they will crave every fleeting project adjournment.

For example, captivating customers with an awe-inspiring advertising campaign may be tasked to a team member with a 'creating' disposition. Weighing up an acquisition opportunity may pass to someone for whom 'judging' is second nature. Explaining to staff how proposed changes will affect their roles might fall to the team member with a gift for 'applying'.

Teams that have been mobilised with care, and granted the luxury of abundant time, are generally able to work to an acceptable level. But strategies can require a faster pace. When exceptional results are demanded, in timescales that have been absurdly concertinaed, teams will need to perform in Power Time.

Power Time means functioning with the intensity of a 100 metre sprinter, making sure that every moment counts. It applies to the sports journalist who must file an evening match report before the presses roll, within 15 minutes of the final whistle. It applies to the newsreader, about to address the nation, who must tear up her script because of breaking news. It applies to the new minister, summoned to give a statement to parliament, who must be in command of a brief and able to handle catcalls and abuse from the other side.

It applies to the barrister preparing his opening statement moments after being updated by the instructing solicitor. And it applies to the partygoer, who may have imbibed a glass or two of rioja, and is suddenly asked to propose a light-hearted vote of thanks to the host in front of 200 guests.

UNLEASHING THE POTENTIAL

When team leaders need their people to find hidden reserves, and excel regardless of the severe time pressure, there are a number of management techniques they can adopt.   The G-Force method (six steps, each beginning with the letter G) was specifically designed for high intensity situations, when all requests for a more forgiving approach to deadlines have been rebuffed from on high. It shifts the mood from "let's start next month" to "we're ready already".

Step one: Gain an anchored mindset. Before rushing headlong into the task, the team consciously readies itself for the performance. Distractions are put aside, focus is achieved, despondency replaced with a willing and gung-ho spirit. Sometimes, leaders might ask each team member to spend a few moments engaged in a personal activity that helps their mental preparations, such as humming a favourite song, meditating, tidying their desk, or indulging in an espresso. With anchored mindsets in place, energies can be positively channelled.

Step two: Go brainstorming. The team thinks laterally about their assigned task. Ideas, facts, opinions and options spew forth expansively. Anything that may have relevance, however tangential, is admitted as a valid contribution.

Every team member is encouraged to participate. If the louder egos start overshadowing the junior or quieter types, the team leader steps in, directing the session so that all voices are heard.

Step three: Generate headlines. From divergence to convergence. The team surveys the results of its brainstorming, and makes the key decisions that will govern the rest of its time together. A mission, a vision, a set of priorities. Standing above detail, the team agrees the handful of achievements that will make it famous; the things which, should a future tabloid editor be composing an attention-grabbing headline, would make the cut.

Step four: Get personal. The team considers the task not as a series of mechanistic actions, but in terms of the impact upon real people, whether customers, staff, suppliers, investors or legislators. If the workplan is too abstract, it is junked. Instead, the team explicitly shapes its programme to be relevant, to deliver benefits that will be tangible and noticed. Significant time may be expended in rapport-building, contextualisation, and empathy. But the result will be a programme that actually matters.

Step five: Give it wings. With the tasks now prioritised and made relevant, the team challenges itself to add a "wow factor". Before moving ahead, the members ask: what is our flash of genius? Our spark of brilliance? How can we move beyond doing a competent job? Where will our audience sit up, mouths agape, at our resolution and enterprise? The team may choose a slogan, a visual, or a killer fact. The point being that exceptional delivery always includes a Red Bull moment.

Step six: Gather and organise. The team assembles all the component pieces into a kit and caboodle ready for delivery. It decides how the 'brainstorming' fits with the 'headlines' fit with the 'personal' fits with the 'wings'. No longer eye-straining at individual pieces of the jigsaw, it concentrates on the whole. The beginning, middle and end. The pace, the timing, the milestones. In a legal firm, step six may see a Term Sheet take shape. In an R&D lab, it may be the full product specification. In a media company, it may be the production sequence. Across all these sectors, remarkable results will not arise unless the team has knitted together a coherent package from all its endeavours.

It was White House chief of staff, Rahm Emanuel, who once said "Don't waste a good crisis", meaning that exceptional times can create the circumstances to get desirable things done. Some teams, delivering strategy under pressure, will be unable to cope. Others will rise up, relishing the chance to discard previous limitations on their abilities. Surrounded by turmoil, they will find the means to simply "do it".

Doing it is the final imperative in battling bloopers. By now, the strategist has worked through 16 risks and temptations, without incident. The situation assessment has been conducted. Core options are understood, and priorities set. Competitors have been evaluated, and customers segmented. Economic and demographic trends are favourable, the government is supportive, and the spirit of innovation is yearning for release. Action plans have been prepared, progress measures agreed, departments aligned, and communications delivered.

Teams are ready to unleash their potential. To triumph. Audacious results are in sight.

Now it is time to create the future.

THE G-FORCE

As well as helping team mobilise to deliver strategic projects, the G-Force method can also be used to prepare short talks on almost any subject, with just six and a half minutes' notice.

At a recent workshop, six career high-flyers were provided with a series of topics that included the cultural influence of Walt Disney, the American space programme, the National Trust, $E=MC^2$, and Corruption. Using the G-Force method, each was tasked to prepare a well-structured after-dinner speech. The talks were videotaped, discussed by the group, and improvements to content and technique highlighted.

As they repeated the exercise, the members of the group became increasingly confident operating under tight deadlines. They avoided awkward blackout moments, were better able to retain their composure in front of an unfamiliar audience, and delivered their remarks in a more authoritative and engaging manner.

SOURCES

Chapter 1: Rees-Mogg, William, *Picnics on Vesuvius*, Sidgwick & Jackson, 1992

Chapter 2: Kast, Fremont and Rosenzweig, James, *Organisation and Management*, McGraw Hill, 1985

Chapter 3: Porter, Michael, *Competitive Strategy*, Free Press, 1980

Chapter 4: Chan Kim, W, and Mauborgne, Renee, *Blue Ocean Strategy*, Harvard Business School Press, 2005

Chapter 5: Ferguson, Niall, *Civilisation: The West and the Rest*, Allen Lane, 2011

Chapter 6: Wayland, Robert and Cole, Paul, *Customer Connections: New Strategies for Growth*, Harvard Business School Press, 1997

Chapter 7: Roberts, Wess, *The Leadership Secrets of Attila The Hun*, Business Plus, 1990. Maude, Francis, ministerial foreward to *Growing the Social Investment Market: A Vision and Strategy*, HM Government, 2011

Chapter 8: Kay, John, *Foundations of Corporate Success*, Oxford University Press, 1993

Chapter 9: Tai, Jacky and Chew, Wilson, *Killer Differentiators*, Marshall Cavendish, 2010. Isaacson, Walter, *Steve Jobs*, Little Brown, 2011

Chapter 10: Reichheld, Frederick, *The Loyalty Effect*, Harvard Business School Press, 1996. Hofstede, Geert, *Culture's Consequences*, Sage Publications, 2001

Chapter 11: Smith, Laurence and Wolfe, David, *A Winning Approach to Strategic Business Planning*, Prime Position Papers, 1993. Hedley, Barry, *Strategy and the Business Portfolio*, Long Range Planning, Pergamon Press, 1977

Chapter 12: Peters, Thomas and Waterman, Robert, *In Search of Excellence*, Harper & Row Publishers, 1982

Chapter 13: Collins, Jim and Porras, Jerry, *Built to Last*, Random House, 1994

Chapter 14: Covey, Stephen, *The Seven Habits of Highly Effective People*, Simon & Schuster, 1992

Chapter 15: Dyson, James, *Against The Odds*, Orion Business Books, 1997

Chapter 16: Kaplan, Robert and Norton, David, *The Balanced Scorecard*, Harvard Business School Press, 1996

Chapter 17: Unpublished Chase Noble report on the G-Force methodology

AVOIDING BLOOPERS
CHECKLIST ☑

- ☐ You need a strategy
- ☐ Engage your people
- ☐ Understand where you are
- ☐ Understand where you want to be
- ☐ Live in the future
- ☐ Customers pay your wages… and have choices
- ☐ Prepare for a warzone
- ☐ Government can make or break you
- ☐ Innovate to survive
- ☐ Success must be sustainable
- ☐ Set priorities
- ☐ Understand how to get there
- ☐ Get your teams aligned
- ☐ Communicate broadly, deeply and often
- ☐ Be flexible; it works for entrepreneurs
- ☐ Measure your progress
- ☐ Do it, in Power Time

cn chasenoble

Chase Noble delivers game-changing strategies for market leaders.

Leadership can take many forms. Customer delight, public reputation, sales, profitability, innovation.

Long-term market leaders possess the ability to game-change ... continually refreshing and revitalising their strategies. Others, once they reach a leadership position, lose the spark that drove their success. They become inflexible, unresponsive and over-cautious.

Chase Noble's approach is to work alongside clients in a results-driven manner. Sometimes, it is the catalyst for identifying new sources of untapped value. At other times, it helps owners and directors to achieve planned benefits faster and with greater ambition.

A number of tested consulting methodologies and analytical models are used, which are designed and delivered in ways that are appropriate to each situation. These include tools to:
- Demonstrate the sources and drivers of value in complex organisations
- Align commercial, technological and organisational objectives
- Identify, manage and mitigate risk
- Set and quantify priorities, giving named executives the accountability and resources to get the job done.

For ten years, Chase Noble has worked with many of Europe's highest profile organisations to achieve and secure market leadership on their own terms.

Chase Noble Ltd
Audley House
Brimpton Common
Berkshire RG7 4RT
United Kingdom
Tel: +44 (0) 118 982 1074
www.chasenoble.com